SHEEP ON THE FARM

Cliff Moon

Illustrated by Anna Jupp

A DOWN ON THE FARM BOOK

THE BOOKWRIGHT PRESS
NEW YORK · 1983

Other books in this series

**DAIRY COWS ON THE FARM
POULTRY ON THE FARM
PIGS ON THE FARM**

Published in the United States in 1983 by
The Bookwright Press, 387 Park Avenue South, New York NY 10016
First published in 1983 by
Wayland Publishers Ltd., England.
© Copyright 1983 Wayland Publishers Ltd.

ISBN: 0-531-04698-2
Library of Congress Catalog Card Number: 83-71628
Printed in Italy by
G. Canale & C.S.p.A., Turin

Contents

Look at the picture.
How many things made from wool
can you see?
There are sweaters, scarves and blankets.
What else is there?
Wool comes from sheep, and
this book is about sheep.

Here are four kinds of sheep.
They all look different, and
their wool is different.
Which sheep do you think
gives the most wool?
(Answer on page 32)

Merino

Romney

Southdown

Leicester

7

Sheep like to live outdoors in fields
or on hills.
These sheep are in a field.
The farmer is looking after them.
The sheepdog runs around the sheep and
keeps them together in a flock.
The farmer whistles and shouts to his dog
to tell him what to do next.

9

This sheep has two baby lambs.
First the farmer and his dog
got all the sheep near to the farm.
Then the lambs were born.
At night the sheepdog has to look after
the lambs because a fox or a coyote might
come and eat them.

11

This lamb is drinking milk from its mother.
The lamb will die if it does not have milk.
Sometimes the sheep does not want her lamb to drink,
and the farmer has to fasten her head in a frame.
Now the lamb can drink all the milk it wants.

The farmer is putting a green mark on the sheep.
Her lamb will have a green mark
in the same place.
If the sheep loses her lamb
the farmer will look at the marks and
find her lamb for her.

Lambs stay near the farm
for a few days after they are born.
Then they go out into the fields
to eat the grass.
These lambs are playing a game that
children call "King of the Castle".
The lamb on top of the straw
tries to push the others off.

17

This sheep is having a bath!
All the sheep have to go through
the *sheep-dip* bath to get rid of insects
which stick to their wool.
One man has a pole to push the sheep
under the wâter.
What do you think the other man
will do with his brush?

(Answer on page 32)

It is summer, and the men are cutting
the wool off the sheep.
They try to get all the wool off
in one piece.
This is called a *fleece*.
They are using electric shears and
they take about four minutes to shear one sheep.
The sheep like it because it makes them cool.

21

The lambs in the field
are waiting for their mothers.
Soon all the sheep will be ready.
They will rush into the field
to find their lambs.
But the sheep look different.
How do you think a lamb will know
which sheep is his mother?
(Answer on page 32)

The men are packing the fleeces into sacks.
They can get 35 fleeces into one sack.
Now the wool is ready to be sold.

Some wool is made into thread and then
woven on a loom like this.
Woolen cloth can be made into dresses or suits.
How do you think the wool became red
and yellow?
(Answer on page 32)

You can buy lamb at the butcher's.
How does it get there?
In autumn when the grass stops growing
the farmer sells some lambs for meat.

In winter the sheep cannot find fresh grass.
Sometimes they eat vegetables instead.
Look at the bottom of the picture.
Wool and meat come from sheep.
And you can make cheese and butter
from sheep's milk and
candles and soap from sheep's fat.

31

Answers to questions

Page 6

The Merino sheep will give the most wool.

Page 18

The other man scrubs the sheep with his brush.

Page 22

The lamb will know which sheep is his mother
when he hears her voice bleating.
Every sheep has a different bleat.

Page 26

The wool became red and yellow
when it was *dyed* those colors.
Wool that is not dyed is gray.

Index